EOIN COLFER'S
ARTEMIS FOWL
THE OPAL DECEPTION

Adapted by
EOIN COLFER
&
ANDREW DONKIN

Art by GIOVANNI RIGANO

Colour by PAOLO LAMANNA
Colour Separation by STUDIO BLINQ

Lettering by CHRIS DICKEY

PUFFIN

PUFFIN BOOKS

Published by the Penguin Group
Penguin Books Ltd, 80 Strand, London WC2R 0RL, England
Penguin Group (USA) Inc., 375 Hudson Street, New York, New York 10014, USA
Penguin Group (Canada), 90 Eglinton Avenue East, Suite 700, Toronto, Ontario,
Canada M4P 2Y3 (a division of Pearson Penguin Canada Inc.)
Penguin Ireland, 25 St Stephen's Green, Dublin 2, Ireland (a division of Penguin Books Ltd)
Penguin Group (Australia), 707 Collins Street, Melbourne, Victoria 3008, Australia
(a division of Pearson Australia Group Pty Ltd)
Penguin Books India Pvt Ltd, 11 Community Centre, Panchsheel Park,
New Delhi – 110 017, India
Penguin Group (NZ), 67 Apollo Drive, Rosedale, Auckland 0632, New Zealand
(a division of Pearson New Zealand Ltd)
Penguin Books (South Africa) (Pty) Ltd, Block D, Rosebank Office Park, 181 Jan Smuts Avenue,
Parktown North, Gauteng 2193, South Africa

Penguin Books Ltd, Registered Offices: 80 Strand, London WC2R 0RL, England

www.puffinbooks.com

Adapted by Eoin Colfer and Andrew Donkin from the novel *Artemis Fowl and the Opal Deception*,
published in Great Britain by Puffin Books

First published in the USA by Disney • Hyperion Books, an imprint of Disney Book Group, 2014
Published in Great Britain by Puffin Books 2014
001

Text copyright © Eoin Colfer, 2014
Illustrations copyright © Giovanni Rigano, 2014
Colour by Paolo Lamanna
Lettering by Chris Dickey
All rights reserved

The moral right of the author and illustrator has been asserted

Printed in Italy by Graphicom

British Library Cataloguing in Publication Data
A CIP catalogue record for this book is available from the British Library

ISBN: 978–0–141–35027–1

www.greenpenguin.co.uk

MIX
Paper from
responsible sources
FSC
www.fsc.org   FSC™ C018179

Penguin Books is committed to a sustainable
future for our business, our readers and our
planet. This book is made from paper certified
by the Forest Stewardship Council.

CHAPTER 1:
TOTALLY OBSESSED

WILL THAT BE ON TONIGHT'S BULLETIN?

TONIGHT'S? YOU GOTTA BE JOKING, DOC. THE ONLY TIME THAT'S EVER GONNA GET SCREENED IS ON THE DAY WHEN NOTHING HAPPENS ANYWHERE IN THE WORLD.

NO OFFENCE, BUT OPAL'S BEEN IN A COMA FOR NEARLY A YEAR. WHETHER SHE'S FAKING IT OR NOT, WATCHING HER DROOL ISN'T EXACTLY A RATINGS WINNER ANY MORE. WE'LL KEEP THAT ON STANDBY AS A PIECE OF FILLER.

OH...

THANKS FOR YOUR TIME THOUGH. AND, HEY, I WAS SORRY TO READ ABOUT YOUR WIFE SUING FOR DIVORCE.

WHAT?

CAN'T BE EASY, HER TELLING EVERYONE YOU NEVER LISTEN TO A WORD SHE SAYS.

MY WIFE IS SUING ME FOR DIVORCE??

SEE YOU LATER, DOC.

DIVORCE...?

EVENING, DR. ARGON.

ERR, EVENING.

UMM, CORPORAL GRUB KELP, ISN'T IT?

GOOD FILM, CORPORAL GRUB?

NOT BAD. HUMAN WESTERN. PLENTY OF SHOOTING AND SQUINTING. YOU CAN BORROW IT IF YOU PROMISE TO KEEP IT IN THE SPECIAL CLOTH.

I'M PICKY ABOUT THAT SORT OF THING.

SAY, DID YOU GET MY LETTER COMPLAINING ABOUT THAT PROTRUDING FLOOR RIVET SCRATCHING MY BOOTS?

I DID INDEED, CORPORAL GRUB. REST ASSURED, I PUT THE LETTER WHERE IT BELONGED.

THANK YOU, SIR.

HOW TO RELEASE A DANGEROUS PSYCHOPATH IN TEN EASY STEPS:

STEP 1: ACTIVATE SONIX REMOTE CONTROL.

OKAY, HERE WE GO.

CLICK!

STEP 2: TRIGGER CHARGE TO BURST BALLOON CONTAINING ACID.

STEP 3: MELT THE CLINIC'S POWER CUBES AND THE BACKUP UNIT.

STEP 4: ENSURE LIGHTS AND ALL SECURITY SYSTEMS ARE OFF-LINE FOR TWO MINUTES.

HEY!

STEP 5: SLIP SEDATIVE PATCH ON TO UNWITTING GUARD.

WHAT'S GOING ON? I'M GONNA...

STEP 6: USE DOOR CODE STOLEN FROM DR. ARGON.

STEP 7: REMOVE SLEEPER TRACER FROM UNDER SKIN. HEAL WOUND WITH MAGIC.

SCALPEL.

STEP 8: WAKE TARGET.

MISS KOBOI?

I'LL JOLT HER.

ZZZZ

~GASP~ CUDGEON!

MISS KOBOI, IT'S US. MERVALL AND DESCANT. IT'S TIME.

"Get the clone."

STEP 9: REPLACE PSYCHOPATH WITH PRE-GROWN CLONE OF PSYCHOPATH.

IDIOTS. ITS EYES ARE OPEN. IT CAN SEE ME!

DON'T WORRY. IT CAN'T TELL ANYONE.

"But its eyes can register images. Foaly may think to check."

"Don't fret, miss. Very soon, that will be the least of Foaly's worries."

STEP 10: IMPLANT SLEEPER TRACER IN CLONE. HEAL WOUND WITH MAGIC.

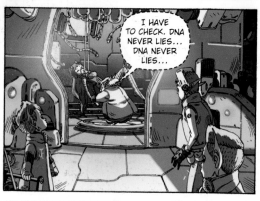

Thieves have their own folklore.

Stories of ingenious heists and death-defying robberies.

Perhaps the most thrilling legend is the tale of the lost Hervé masterpiece.

CHAPTER 2:
THE FAIRY THIEF

Every schoolboy knows that Pascal Hervé was the French Impressionist who painted extraordinarily beautiful pictures of the fairy folk.

And every art dealer knows that Hervé's fifteen fairy paintings command sums of over 50 million Euros each.

In the upper criminal echelons there were always rumours of a secret, final, sixteenth painting. Entitled "The Fairy Thief", it is said to depict a fairy in the act of stealing a human child.

Legend has it that Hervé gave the painting to a beautiful Turkish girl he met on the Champs-Elysées.

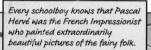

The girl promptly broke Hervé's heart and sold the picture to an English tourist for twenty francs. Within weeks, the picture had been stolen from the Englishman's home.

"The Fairy Thief" has become something of a trophy for top thieves worldwide.

Since that time, it's believed the painting has been stolen fifteen times. What is unique is that each time the thief decided to keep the painting.

Whoever manages to steal the lost painting is acknowledged as the master thief of his generation.

I am Artemis Fowl the Second.

I am fourteen years old. I am a genius.

For as long as I can remember, I have been fascinated by fairies. I do not know why.

If I succeed, I will be the youngest thief to have ever stolen "The Fairy Thief".

If.

STEP 1: GAIN ENTRY WITH FAKE PASSPORT.

COLONEL LEE, OF COURSE, COME THIS WAY.

AND IS THIS YOUR... SON?

UNFORTUNATELY, DUDE, YES.

MY SON DOES NOT COMMUNICATE WELL WITH THE REST OF THE WORLD.

I HAVE A GIRL. SIXTEEN YEARS OLD. TEENAGERS, THEY'RE ALL THE...

ALFONSE!

POP!

THIS ELEVATOR IS THE ONLY WAY IN AND OUT OF OUR VAULT.

THAT'S SO EXCITING, DUDE, I THINK I MIGHT FAINT.

STEP 2: SMUGGLE IN SPECIALIST EQUIPMENT.

WHAT IS THIS?

IT'S A SCOOTER, DUDE. YOU KNOW, TRANSPORTATION THAT DOESN'T POLLUTE THE AIR.

HE'S CLEAN.

BEEEEP!

HE'S GOT METAL ON HIS PERSON.

STEP 3: SMUGGLE IN METAL KEYS.

YOU'RE NOT, LIKE, GONNA MAKE ME RIP MY BRACES OUT, ARE YOU, DUDE?

PLEASE TURN THE KEY WHEN I DO, COLONEL. THEY MUST BE TURNED EXACTLY TOGETHER.

I'LL LEAVE YOU TO YOUR BUSINESS.

THANK YOU, BERTHOLT.

STEP 4: OPEN ARCHITECT'S DRAWING TO BLOCK CAMERA VIEW.

RAISE YOUR ARMS HIGHER AND TAKE A STEP TO THE LEFT.

"PERFECT."

STEP 5: USE X-RAY SCANNER DISGUISED AS VIDEO GAME TO LOCATE THE CORRECT BOX.

WE RENTED OUR OWN BOX ONLY TWO DAYS AFTER THEY DID, SO THEY SHOULD BE CLOSE TOGETHER, WHICH MEANS SOMEWHERE...

...HERE. I THINK THIS COULD BE IT BUTLER.

STEP 6: LOCATE THE LOCKSMITH'S SIGNATURE.

BLOKKEN

STEP 7: RETRIEVE MASTER KEYS ALLOWED THROUGH METAL DETECTOR.

STEP 8: USE SPECIALLY ADAPTED SCOOTER COLUMN TO TURN TWO KEYS AT SAME TIME.

HERE WE GO...

YES!

CLICK

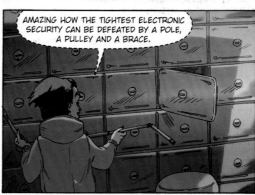

AMAZING HOW THE TIGHTEST ELECTRONIC SECURITY CAN BE DEFEATED BY A POLE, A PULLEY AND A BRACE.

STEP 9: CHECK DEPOSIT BOX FOR BOOBY TRAPS.

HA—A CIRCUIT BREAKER ATTACHED TO A PORTABLE KLAXON.

HOW EMBARRASSING FOR ANY THIEF TO GET CAUGHT LIKE THAT. SOMEONE HAS A SENSE OF HUMOUR.

STEP 10: DISCONNECT BOOBY TRAP.

ARE WE DONE, ARTEMIS? MY ARMS ARE GETTING RATHER TIRED.

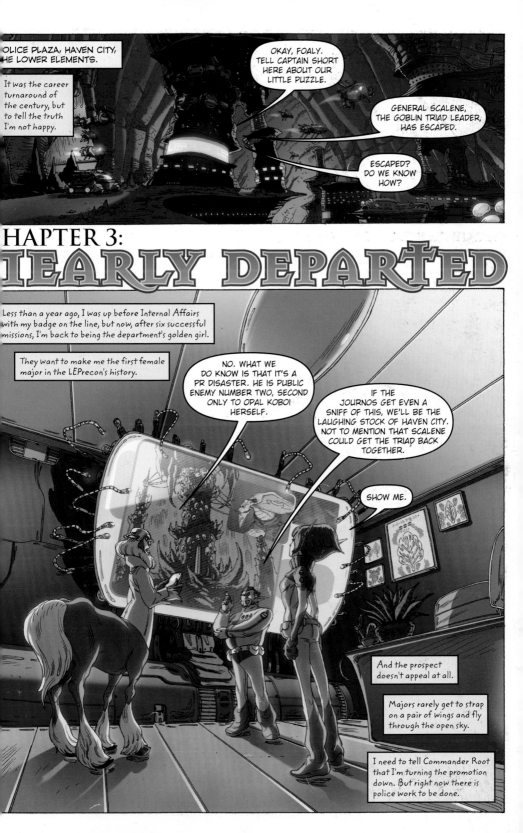

POLICE PLAZA, HAVEN CITY, THE LOWER ELEMENTS.

It was the career turnaround of the century, but to tell the truth I'm not happy.

OKAY, FOALY. TELL CAPTAIN SHORT HERE ABOUT OUR LITTLE PUZZLE.

GENERAL SCALENE, THE GOBLIN TRIAD LEADER, HAS ESCAPED.

ESCAPED? DO WE KNOW HOW?

CHAPTER 3:
NEARLY DEPARTED

Less than a year ago, I was up before Internal Affairs with my badge on the line, but now, after six successful missions, I'm back to being the department's golden girl.

They want to make me the first female major in the LEPrecon's history.

NO. WHAT WE DO KNOW IS THAT IT'S A PR DISASTER. HE IS PUBLIC ENEMY NUMBER TWO, SECOND ONLY TO OPAL KOBOI HERSELF.

IF THE JOURNOS GET EVEN A SNIFF OF THIS, WE'LL BE THE LAUGHING STOCK OF HAVEN CITY. NOT TO MENTION THAT SCALENE COULD GET THE TRIAD BACK TOGETHER.

SHOW ME.

And the prospect doesn't appeal at all.

Majors rarely get to strap on a pair of wings and fly through the open sky.

I need to tell Commander Root that I'm turning the promotion down. But right now there is police work to be done.

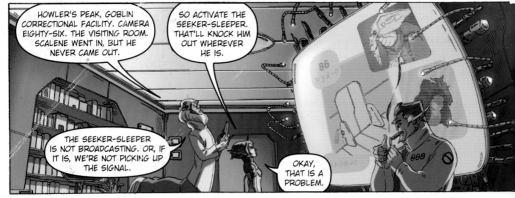

HOWLER'S PEAK, GOBLIN CORRECTIONAL FACILITY. CAMERA EIGHTY-SIX. THE VISITING ROOM. SCALENE WENT IN, BUT HE NEVER CAME OUT.

SO ACTIVATE THE SEEKER-SLEEPER. THAT'LL KNOCK HIM OUT WHEREVER HE IS.

THE SEEKER-SLEEPER IS NOT BROADCASTING. OR, IF IT IS, WE'RE NOT PICKING UP THE SIGNAL.

OKAY, THAT IS A PROBLEM.

SO WHO WAS VISITING GENERAL SCALENE?

ONE OF HIS THOUSAND NEPHEWS, A GOBLIN CALLED BOOHN. HERE'S THE VIDEO OF BOOHN CHECKING IN.

THE VISITOR'S LIST HAS BOOHN ARRIVING AT SEVEN FIFTY. AND THEN CHECKING OUT AT EIGHT FIFTEEN.

HE PASSES THE INTERNAL SECURITY CAMERAS AND THEN HEADS FOR HIS CAR.

08:15 am

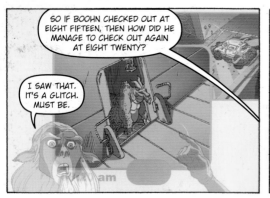

SO IF BOOHN CHECKED OUT AT EIGHT FIFTEEN, THEN HOW DID HE MANAGE TO CHECK OUT AGAIN AT EIGHT TWENTY?

I SAW THAT. IT'S A GLITCH. MUST BE.

EVERYONE WHO ENTERS OR LEAVES HOWLER'S PEAK IS SCANNED A DOZEN TIMES BY FACIAL RECOGNITION SOFTWARE.

I CREATED IT AND THERE'S NO WAY TO FOOL IT.

IF THE COMPUTER SAY IT WAS BOOHN THAT LEFT, THE THAT'S WHO IT WAS.

FOALY, CAN YOU ENLARGE HIS HEAD? SHARPEN THE IMAGE? SHOW ME BOOHN GOING IN AND THE OTHER SHOT OF HIM COMING OUT.

WHAT ARE YOU LOOKING FOR, CAPTAIN?

I DON'T KNOW. SOMETHING. ANYTHING.

My intuition is buzzir like a swarm of bees.

"Look, here's scale blister. Now look at the exit film. No blister."

"So, he burst the blister. Big deal."

"No, it's more than that."

GOING IN, BOOHN'S SKIN IS ALMOST GREY. COMING OUT HE'S BRIGHT GREEN.

WHAT'S YOUR POINT, CAPTAIN?

BOOHN SHED HIS SKIN IN THE VISITOR'S ROOM. SO WHERE'S THE SKIN?

Foaly pulls up footage of the first "Boohn" leaving the visitor's room. It looks a lot like Boohn, but at high magnification it's clear that the goblin's skin is ill-fitting.

Patches are missing and the goblin seems to be holding folds together.

THIS WAS ALL PLANNED. BOOHN WAITS UNTIL HE'S SHEDDING. THEN HE VISITS HIS UNCLE AND THEY PEEL OFF HIS SKIN.

GENERAL SCALENE PUTS ON THE SKIN AND JUST WALKS OUT THE DOOR, FOOLING FOALY'S AUTOMATIC SCANNERS ON THE WAY.

WE NEED TO CATCH SCALENE AND FIND OUT WHO PLANNED THIS.

WHOEVER IT IS, AT LEAST IT'S NOT OPAL. THIS IS A LIVE FEED AND SHE'S STILL IN DREAMY DREAMLAND.

SIR. MAJOR KELP REPORTS THAT HE'S LOCATED GENERAL SCALENE.

HE'S IN CHUTE E37, SIR. AND HE'S ASKING FOR YOU.

WHAT?

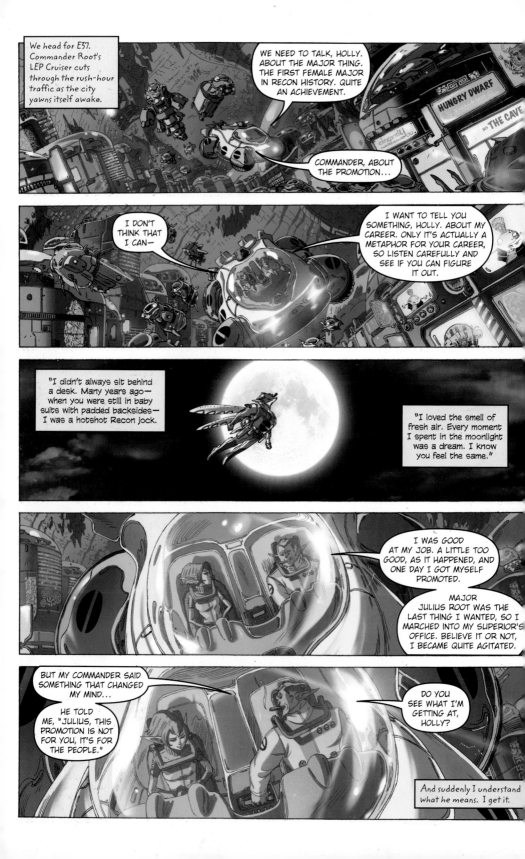

CHUTE E37, HAVEN CITY.

Major Trouble Kelp (Corporal Grub's big brother) briefs us on the situation.

THERMAL SCANS SHOW SCALENE IS ALONE IN THERE. HE LEFT THIS RECORDING FOR US TO FIND.

Root, I would speak to you. I would tell you a great secret. Bring the female, Holly Short. Two only. No more or many will die.

GOBLINS. DRAMA QUEENS, THE LOT OF THEM.

IT'S A TRAP, COMMANDER. WE WERE THE ONES AT KOBOI LABS. THE GOBLINS BLAME US FOR THE REBELLION'S FAILURE. IF WE GO IN THERE, WHO KNOWS WHAT'S WAITING FOR US.

NOW YOU'RE THINKING LIKE A MAJOR.

I'M TEMPTED TO SEND IN TACTICAL AND TAKE A CHANCE THAT HE'S BLUFFING.

THAT WOULD BE MY ADVICE. WE CAN HAVE SCALENE IN A WAGON BEFORE HE CAN LICK HIS OWN EYELIDS.

Root punches his palm with a fist. I know what's ...ing and he's right.

I'M GOING IN. WE CAN'T TAKE A CHANCE WITH OTHER PEOPLE'S LIVES.

My stomach lurches, but I swallow the fear.

Foaly techs us up.

New Neutrino handguns coded to our DNA and linked to the LEP computer.

Next-generation recon suits. The fabric is woven from cam foil so we're virtually hidden all the time. The flying wings are built into the suit.

YOU DON'T HAVE TO DO THIS, YOU KNOW, CAPTAIN.

NO, COMMANDER. THIS IS EXACTLY WHAT I HAVE TO DO.

This is what being an LEP officer is all about. Protecting the People.

The access tunnel smells like a blast furnace.

Ancient swirls of melted ore hang from the roof.

A set of footprints in the deep soot leads us towards...

...THERE.

ON YOUR FEET, SCALENE.

He doesn't move.

I SAID GET UP AND... OH.

HE'S BEEN MESMERIZED.

That means that someone else planned his escape. And worse: we've just walked into a trap.

WE SHOULD GO, COMMANDER, RIGHT AWAY.

NOW THAT WE'RE HERE, WE TAKE SCALENE WITH US.

My soldier's sense is buzzing like crazy.

Don't touch me, Elf.

WHAT?

That voice. I know that voice...

There's a metal box strapped to Scalene's chest. On the small screen at the centre is...

...OPAL KOBOI.

Ah, Julius. I knew your ego wouldn't allow you to stay out of the action. An obvious trap and you walk straight into it.

Things. Are. Going. Terribly. Terribly. Wrong.

FOALY, WE HAVE A SITUATION HERE. *OPAL KOBOI IS LOOSE!* I REPEAT, LOOSE. PUT OUT A CITYWIDE ALERT. *FOALY?*

Talk all you want, Captain Short. Foaly can't hear you. My device is blocking your transmissions as I blocked your seeker-sleeper earlier.

I point my helmet camera. Foaly will see it's her and work out the rest.

Oh, very good, Captain. You were always a smart one Relatively speaking, of course

Sorry to disappoint you, but this entire device is made of stealth ore and is practically invisible. All Foaly will see is a slight shimmer of interference.

The blast doors slam shut behind us.

WE'RE COMPLETELY CUT OFF FROM THE LEP.

SLAMMM!

Alone at last.

WE HAVE TO GET OUT OF HERE. THE CHUTE IS THE ONLY WAY.

AGREED. YOU SINK A FEW CHARGES INTO THE BOX ON SCALENE'S CHEST. I'LL THROW HIM OVER MY SHOULDER AND WE ESCAPE UP E37.

My helmet's air-conditioned, but sometimes sweating has nothing to do with temperature.

I can't help but wonder, is this exactly what Opal wants us to do?

Have we come up with a little plan to...

BDAM BDAM BDAM!

Root leans down and grabs Scalene. Nothing happens. Maybe I'm wrong. Maybe Opal has no plan.

Then suddenly the octo-bonds holding the screen let go of Scalene and whiplash round Commander Root.

AGGGH!

Looks like you're the sacrifice, Commander Root.

D'ARVIT!

I hear a rib crack. Blue sparks of magic start to heal it.

I move to help, but there's an urgent beeping from the device.

STAY BACK; IT'S A PROXIMITY TRIGGER.

Listen to him, Captain Short. If you come too close, he will be vaporized by the explosives now strapped to his chest.

FOALY'S WATCHING THIS. HE'LL FIND US A WAY OUT.

"Ha—Foaly *is* watching and probably wondering why you're pointing a gun at your commanding officer. Remember Foaly can't hear anything and he can't see my screen."

A digital readout flicks into life on Root's chest. A six and a zero.

Once I start the countdown, you have one minute to live, Commander. How does that feel?

Opal's snide laugh rills into my brain.

SHUT IT DOWN, KOBOI. OR I SWEAR I'LL...

Root is already dead. At least save the Mud Men?

Mud Men? Of course. Artemis and Butler. The two other people who helped stop Koboi's plan.

At this very moment, young Artemis is stealing a package from the International Bank in Munich.

He believes it contains a valuable painting. It does. It also contains a homing chip for a bio-bomb.

"You can stay here and attempt to explain all this. It shouldn't take more than a few hours. Or you can try to keep your friends alive."

I WILL HUNT YOU DOWN, KOBOI. FOR YOU, THERE WON'T BE A SAFE INCH ON THE PLANET.

Such venom. What if I start the countdown, but give you a sporting chance to save your beloved commanding officer?

There's a sweet spot on the device. Two-centimetre diameter. It's the red spot on the screen.

Hit that from outside the trigger area and you overload the circuit.

There's nothing I can do.

BOOOOMMMM!

For the briefest moment the particles twinkle...

...like a million gold stars falling to earth.

Then he's gone.

Commander Root is gone.

— BREAKING NEWS — COMMANDER ROOT
BELIEVED KILLED IN EXPLOSION IN
CHUTE E37 — BREAKING NEWS —

—MEMO—

FROM: EDITOR-IN-CHIEF
TO: NEWSROOM STAFF

If this terrible news is true then
we're going to need wall-to-wall
coverage of this tragic (and potentiall
ratings-increasing) event.

TO-DO LIST

1. Get a camera crew over to chute E37 and
   another to Police Plaza.

2. Pull all archive files on Commander Root and
   his decades in charge of the LEPrecon unit.

3. Find out who sold him those noxious fungus
   cigars and interview them—adds character.

4. Avoid all mention of his brother, Turnball Root.
   Best not to drag that low-life criminal into this
   story. Keep it heroic.

5. Why are you still reading this? Get out there
   and get me this story!

6. Err . . . And find out how he died!?

MUNICH.

The container could easily be booby-trapped, so I must wait until I am back in my room to open it safely.

The journey back to the hotel should take twenty minutes. Rush-hour traffic means it takes nearly two hours.

I use the time wisely.

I ring my mother.

HAPTER 4:
IARROW ESCAPES

DON'T YOU THINK THAT JUST ONCE YOU COULD CALL ME "MUM"; WOULD THAT BE SO TERRIBLE?

I'M WORRIED ABOUT YOU, ARTY. SOMEONE YOUR AGE SHOULDN'T BE SO... RESPONSIBLE. I HOPE PRINCIPAL GUINEY IS LOOKING AFTER YOU.

I AM FOURTEEN NOW, REMEMBER?

I tell Mother that I have a twenty-four-hour tummy bug. We talk. She says everything I need to hear.

open an audio manipulation program n my laptop and get to work. I cut nd paste Mother's words into a new essage. When I'm done I ring Principal uiney's message service.

"Principal Guiney, I'm worried about Arty. He has a tummy bug and we want him home with us. You understand. I have put Arty on a plane. We will talk more on your return."

That takes care of school for a few days.

Part of me feels an electric thrill at the subterfuge, but my growing conscience feels guilty at using Mother's voice to tell my lies.

As for stealing "The Fairy Thief"...theft from thieves is surely not even a crime.

Yes, says a voice in the back of my head, especially if you give the painting back to the world.

In the privacy of my hotel room, I get to work.

The first task is to check the container for poison gas.

Sample contains oxygen, hydrogen, methane, carbon dioxide, and one unidentified inert gas. Sample is nontoxic.

I tease the painting from the cylinder and unroll it.

The figures are painted so beautifully they seem to sparkle.

I know immediately... this is no fake.

THE FAIRY CAN'T GO INSIDE...

The fairy is perched on the windowsill because it can't go inside without an invitation.

How do I know that?

CRRRRRASHHH!

As we fall, I see
an iridescent blue
flash above us.

Bio-bomb.
Now, how do
I know that?

Once again, Butler
has saved my life.

I try to move, but I feel a broken rib break through
my skin. Suddenly a red stain blossoms on my
shirt and everything around me fades to black.

It takes me almost ninety minutes to reach Munich.

m seconds away from saving rtemis when I see the blue flash.

I'm too late and the realization hits me hard. Opal has set me up again.

here was never any hope of aving Artemis, just as there was never any hope of saving Commander Root.

Julius is gone.

Artemis is dead.

Butler is dead.

What point is there in going on?

SHE'S WON. OPAL HAS WON.

I have to get up. I am an LEP officer.

There is more at stake here than my personal grieving.

I don't move. I feel like grief has scooped out my insides. I'm hollow and utterly lost.

How very touching...

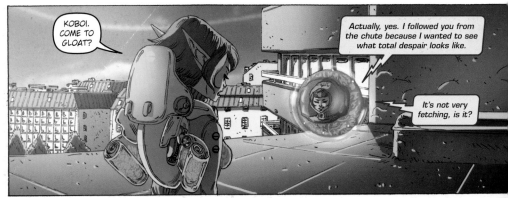

KOBOI. COME TO GLOAT?

Actually, yes. I followed you from the chute because I wanted to see what total despair looks like.

It's not very fetching, is it?

DETONATE AND GET IT OVER WITH.

Oh, I will. But it's what happens after that's important.

DON'T TELL ME, KOBOI: WORLD DOMINATION.

World domination? You make it sound so unattainable. The first step is simplicity itself. All I have to do is put humans in contact with the People.

The LEP studied me like an animal in a cage. Now let's see how they like it.

ALL THIS FOR A CHILDISH PIXIE'S REVENGE?

Oh I'm not a pixie any more. Look...no pointy ears. I intend to be on the winning side once that probe goes down.

WHAT PROBE?

Enough explaining. You cost me a year of my life, Short. A year.

On the screen I see the hatred in Opal's eyes. Then she holds up a small remote and presses the button.

I have seconds before the bio-bomb explodes.

The killing agent in a bio-bomb is solinium, and LEP helmets are supposed to be able to deflect solinium flares.

Let's see if they can.

I hook my helmet over the bomb and point it away from me.

Pale blue light gushes from the underside of the helmet...spreading death.

I hold on for as long as I can, until the concussion wave throws me off.

The helmet spins away and the lethal light is free.

I flip my wing control and head towards the sky.

It's a race now.

The bio-bomb blast rises like a wall of death and I have to outrun it.

G-forces ripple my cheeks.

The blue light gains and a dreadful feeling of nothingness creeps up my legs.

I streamline my body to climb.

My wings begin to overheat when suddenly the light flashes out and disappears.

I've done it.

I've survived.

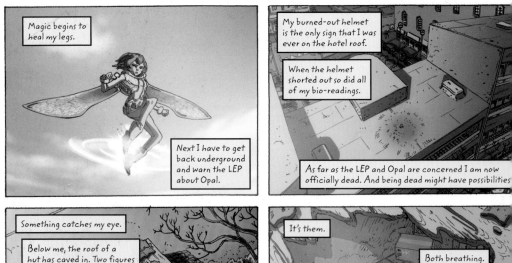

Magic begins to heal my legs.

Next I have to get back underground and warn the LEP about Opal.

My burned-out helmet is the only sign that I was ever on the hotel roof.

When the helmet shorted out so did all of my bio-readings.

As far as the LEP and Opal are concerned I am now officially dead. And being dead might have possibilities

Something catches my eye.

Below me, the roof of a hut has caved in. Two figures are lying in the remains.

Please. Please.

It's them.

Both breathing.

There's blood everywhere and Artemis is going into shock. I have to be fast.

I heal them both.

Butler is simply too bulky to move.

GOODBYE, OLD FRIEND. I'LL BE BACK FOR YOU.

I hate to leave him but I have to get Artemis to safety.

If Opal insists on joining the world of men, then Artemis is surely the ideal foil for her genius.

I shield Artemis as best I can and open the throttle on my wings.

E37, THE LOWER ELEMENTS.

HEY, CENTAUR, YOU LISTENING?

YOU LOOK LIKE YOUR BRAIN HAS GONE INTO DEEP FREEZE.

MEET THE NEIGHBOURS

CHAPTER 5:

COMMANDER ARK SOOL— HIGHEST-RANKING GNOME IN INTERNAL AFFAIRS.

IT'S NO SECRET I THINK THE LEP IS BASICALLY A BUNCH OF LOOSE CANNONS, PRESIDED OVER BY A MAVERICK. AND NOW THAT MAVERICK IS DEAD, APPARENTLY KILLED BY THE BIGGEST LOOSE CANNON IN THE BUNCH.

HOLLY SHORT HAS NARROWLY AVOIDED CRIMINAL CHARGES TWICE IN HER CAREER. SHE WON'T ESCAPE THIS TIME.

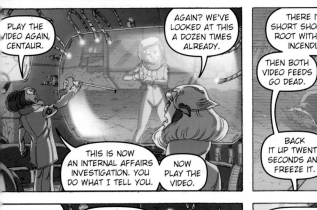

PLAY THE VIDEO AGAIN, CENTAUR.

AGAIN? WE'VE LOOKED AT THIS A DOZEN TIMES ALREADY.

THIS IS NOW AN INTERNAL AFFAIRS INVESTIGATION. YOU DO WHAT I TELL YOU.

NOW PLAY THE VIDEO.

THERE IT IS. CAPTAIN SHORT SHOOTS COMMANDER ROOT WITH SOME SORT OF INCENDIARY BULLET.

THEN BOTH VIDEO FEEDS GO DEAD.

BACK IT UP TWENTY SECONDS AND FREEZE IT.

WHAT IS THAT? THAT SHIMMER ON ROOT'S CHEST?

I'M NOT SURE. HEAT DISTORTION? DIGITAL GLITCH?

I CAN RUN SOME TESTS.

WHATEVER IT IS, SHORT'S A BURNOUT. SHE ALWAYS WAS.

I NEARLY HAD HER BEFORE, BUT THIS TIME IT'S CUT-AND-DRIED.

ISN'T THIS ALL A BIT CONVENIENT?

I MEAN, FIRST WE LOSE SOUND, SO WE DON'T KNOW WHAT'S SAID. THEN THERE'S A FUZZY PATCH THAT COULD BE ANYTHING.

NOW WE'RE EXPECTED TO BELIEVE THAT A DECORATED OFFICER JUST UP AND SHOT HER COMMANDER.

JULIUS WAS LIKE A FATHER TO HER.

I SEE YOUR POINT, FOALY. NICE TO KNOW YOUR BRAIN IS STILL WORKING.

THE PROBLEM IS, THE SHOTS FIRED ON THE VIDEO EXACTLY MATCH THE WEAPON'S LOG.

WHATEVER ELSE HAPPENED IN THAT CHUTE, SHORT FIRED ON HER COMMANDING OFFICER.

BUT HOLLY'S WEAPON FIRING SHOULDN'T HAVE CAUSED SUCH A HUGE EXPLOSION. IT PRACTICALLY CAVED IN THE WHOLE CHUTE.

I'M SURE THERE'S AN EXPLANATION. COMBUSTIBLE GAS OR SOMETHING. BUT FOR NOW MY PRIORITY, AND *YOURS*, IS TO BRING BACK CAPTAIN SHORT FOR TRIAL.

TELL ME THIS: IF SHE'S INNOCENT, THEN WHY DID SHE RUN? THE RETRIEVAL TEAM WILL BRING HER BACK.

WHERE IS SHE NOW?

SHE REACHED MUNICH, GERMANY, A FEW MINUTES AGO. SHE HASN'T MOVED FOR A...

WHAT JUST HAPPENED?

OH NO. THE LIFE SIGNS FROM HOLLY'S HELMET JUST FLATLINED.

COULD SHE HAVE JUST TAKEN IT OFF?

NO, THERE'S AN INFRARED LINK BETWEEN HER AND THE HELMET. SOMETHING TERRIBLE JUST HAPPENED.

ACTIVATE THE SELF-DESTRUCT UNIT IN HER HELMET. AND RECALL THE RETRIEVAL TEAM.

CAPTAIN SHORT WAS A TRAITOR. SHE MUST HAVE BEEN IN COLLUSION WITH THE GOBLINS. HER PLAN BACKFIRED AND SHE GOT HERSELF KILLED.

BUT...

I'M SORRY, FOALY. JUST DO IT. I'M AFRAID YOUR FRIEND HOLLY SHORT IS HISTORY.

VERY WELL. I DON'T REMEMBER ANY OF THIS, BUT I DO BELIEVE YOU. I ACCEPT THAT WE HUMANS HAVE FAIRY NEIGHBOURS BELOW THE PLANET'S SURFACE.

JUST LIKE THAT?

HARDLY. BUT I HAVE TAKEN YOUR STORY AND CROSS-REFERENCED IT WITH THE FACTS AS I KNOW THEM.

YOUR STORY FITS, RIGHT DOWN TO SOMETHING THAT YOU COULD NOT POSSIBLY KNOW ABOUT, CAPTAIN SHORT.

"A while ago, I discovered mirrored contact lenses in my own eyes, as well as Butler's and Juliet's."

"Investigation revealed that I myself ordered them, although I have no memory of that fact. I now suspect I ordered them to cheat your *mesmer*."

I MUST HAVE PLANTED A TRIGGER SOMEWHERE. SOMETHING THAT WOULD MAKE ME REMEMBER. BUT WHAT?

I HAVE NO IDEA. I WAS HOPING THAT JUST SEEING ME WOULD TRIGGER A RECALL.

THE ONLY WAY MY MEMORIES WILL BE RETURNED TO ME IS IF THE ONE PERSON I TRUST COMPLETELY AND UTTERLY PRESENTED ME WITH IRREFUTABLE EVIDENCE.

I feel myself growing annoyed. I am reminded that Artemis can get under my skin like nobody else.

AND WHO IS THIS ONE PERSON WHOM YOU COMPLETELY AND UTTERLY TRUST?

WHY, MYSELF, OF COURSE.

MUNICH.

EXCUSE ME, ARE YOU ALIVE?

I AM ALIVE. WHERE IS THE BOY WHO WAS WITH ME?

BOY? THERE IS NO BOY.

OF COURSE, THERE WAS NO BOY.

FORGIVE ME; THE MIND TENDS TO WANDER AFTER A THREE-STOREY FALL.

"Artemis, I'm assuming you are alive and I am leaving this message on your mobile phone. If you've been kidnapped the kidnappers will contact Fowl Manor with their demands."

"If you've simply removed yourself from danger then you will head for home."

"Either way, the trail leads to Fowl Manor and that's where I'm heading now."

TEMPLE BAR, DUBLIN, IRELAND.

WHAT IS THIS PLACE? SOME FORM OF SURVEILLANCE HIDE?

EXACTLY. I WAS ON STAKEOUT HERE A FEW MONTHS AGO. ROGUE DWARFS FENCING STOLEN JEWELLERY.

FROM THE OUTSIDE, THIS IS JUST ANOTHER PATC OF SKY ON TOP OF A BUILDING. IT'S A CHAM POD.

YOU'RE TAKING ALL THIS VERY CALMLY.

MOST HUMANS COMPLETELY FREAK OUT WHEN THEY FIND OUT ABOUT THE PEOPLE. SOME GO INTO SHOCK.

I AM NOT MOST HUMANS.

I've known Artemis for several years, and I'm certainly not going to argue with that statement.

SO TELL ME, CAPTAIN SHORT. IF ALL I AM TO THE FAIRY PEOPLE IS A THREAT, WHY DID YOU HEAL ME?

IT'S OUR NATURE. AND OF COURSE I NEED YOU TO HELP ME DEFEAT OPAL KOBOI. WE'VE DONE IT BEFORE; WE CAN DO IT AGAIN.

SO FIRST YOU MIND-WIPE ME, AND NOW YOU NEED ME?

YES, ARTEMIS. GLOAT ALL YOU LIKE. THE MIGHTY LEP NEEDS YOUR HELP.

IN THAT CASE, LET'S DISCUSS MY FEE.

FEE? AFTER ALL THAT THE FAIRY FOLK HAVE DONE FOR YOU?

I THINK A PLAN THAT DEFEATS OPAL KOBOI IS WORTH ONE TON OF GOLD, DON'T YOU?

YOU ARE EXACTLY AS YOU WERE WHEN WE FIRST MET, A GREEDY MUD BOY WHO DOESN'T CARE ABOUT ANYONE EXCEPT HIMSELF.

It would be stupid not to ask for a fee. But doing so makes me feel horribly guilty.

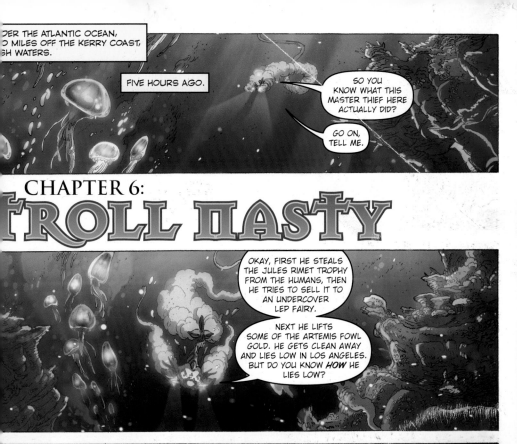

UNDER THE ATLANTIC OCEAN, 80 MILES OFF THE KERRY COAST, IRISH WATERS.

FIVE HOURS AGO.

SO YOU KNOW WHAT THIS MASTER THIEF HERE ACTUALLY DID?

GO ON, TELL ME.

CHAPTER 6:
TROLL NASTY

OKAY, FIRST HE STEALS THE JULES RIMET TROPHY FROM THE HUMANS, THEN HE TRIES TO SELL IT TO AN UNDERCOVER LEP FAIRY.

NEXT HE LIFTS SOME OF THE ARTEMIS FOWL GOLD. HE GETS CLEAN AWAY AND LIES LOW IN LOS ANGELES. BUT DO YOU KNOW *HOW* HE LIES LOW?

HE BUYS HIMSELF A PENTHOUSE APARTMENT AND STARTS STEALING ACADEMY AWARDS. NATURALLY, HE GETS HIMSELF CAUGHT AGAIN.

HA HA HA! WHAT A BRAIN! HOW DOES IT FIT INSIDE HIS ITTY-BITTY HEAD?

LEP-SHUTTLE B-24-08 TRANSPORTING DWARF FELON 1964 — MULCH DIGGUMS.

LAUGH ALL YOU LIKE, FISHBOY. BY TONIGHT, I'LL BE FREE AND EATING ONE OF YOUR COUSINS FOR DINNER.

OH YEAH, MULCH, WHAT WILL YOU DO WHEN YOUR APPEAL IS TURNED DOWN? YOU GONNA CRACK UP LIKE A LITTLE GIRL OR TAKE IT REAL STOIC?

THE DATES ON THOSE SEARCH WARRANTS WERE ALL WRONG. ALL THAT STANDS BETWEEN ME AND SWEET FREEDOM IS A THIRTY-MINUTE INTERVIEW WITH JULIUS ROOT AND THEN I'M WALKING OUTTA HERE.

BEEP BEEP BEEP

YOU REALLY BELIEVE THAT, DON'T YOU, YOU CRAZY DWARF?

LET'S JUST SAY I GOT SOME REAL SMART FRIENDS IN LOW PLACES FRIENDS THAT TAKE CARE OF ME.

EVEN IF YOU DO GET OUT, HOW LONG BEFORE YOU'RE CAUGHT AGAIN, MULCH?

YOUR CRIMINAL CAREER HASN'T EXACTLY BEEN AN UNQUALIFIED SUCCESS.

YEAH, WELL...MAYBE YOU'RE RIGHT. MAYBE IT IS TIME FOR ME TO GO STRAIGHT. YOU KNOW, WHILE I STILL HAVE MY LOOKS.

OF COURSE, WE'LL RETURN TO BAS IMMEDIATELY WITH THE PRISONER.

VISHBY? WHAT'S...?

LOOKS LIKE YOU'LL BE STUCK IN THE DEEPS PRISON FOR A WHILE LONGER, MULCH. TERRIBLE NEWS, COMMANDER ROOT HAS BEEN MURDERED.

JULIUS... GONE?

HOW?

EXPLOSION. APPARENTLY HE WAS MURDERED B ANOTHER LEP OFFICE SHE'S NOW MISSIN PRESUMED DEAD. A CAPTAIN HOLLY SHORT.

WHAT?!

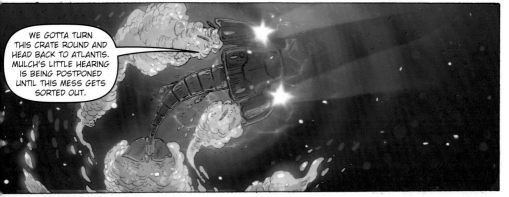

WE GOTTA TURN THIS CRATE ROUND AND HEAD BACK TO ATLANTIS. MULCH'S LITTLE HEARING IS BEING POSTPONED UNTIL THIS MESS GETS SORTED OUT.

HOLLY MURDERS JULIUS.

IT'S NOT POSSIBLE.

THERE'S A CHANCE HOLLY IS STILL ALIVE AND NEEDS MY HELP. FRIENDS, EH? I'M SORRY, FELLAS, I GOTTA GET OUT OF HERE.

YEAH, RIGHT. GOOD LUCK WITH THAT.

YOU MIGHT WANT TO RETIRE TO THE CABIN, BOYS. FOR THE LAST TEN MINUTES I'VE BEEN SUCKING THE AIR OUT OF HERE AND STORING IT IN MY INTESTINES.

WHAT?

WEIRD SECRET DWARF ABILITY.

HE'S KIDDING, RIGHT?

ERR...HE'S *NOT* KIDDING. WE NEED TO MOVE TO THE CABIN.

SHE'S GONNA FOLD!

NOW.

FOWL MANOR, IRELAND.

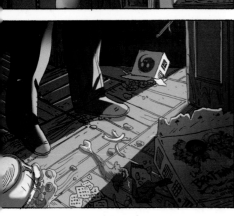

...at the Eleven Wonders, but I've decided you are worthy of it yourself...

THAT FIRST HALF IS A MESSAGE FROM ARTEMIS; THEN IT SOUNDS LIKE OPAL CAPTURED HIM AND HOLLY.

BUT HEY, AT LEAST THAT MEANS HOLLY'S ALIVE, RIGHT?

ELVES?

MAYBE THIS WILL OPEN YOUR MIND? WHEN ARTEMIS GAVE IT TO ME IT WAS PAINTED TO LOOK LIKE A GOLD COIN.

I HANDLED IT SO MUCH THAT SOME OF THE GOLD FLAKED OFF AND I SAW WHAT IT REALLY WAS.

A COMPUTER DISK. IT HAS TO BE A MESSAGE.

ELVES?

COME ON, BIG GUY. JUST PLAY THE DISK.

Hello, Butler. If you are watching this then our dear friend Mister Diggums has come through. There is also a strong possibility that you are watching this at a time of peril, so I'll be brief.

Fairies are real and some of them are our friends.

In order to verify the fantastic facts I am about to reveal, I will say one word. Just one. A word that bodyguard etiquette forbids me to know...unless you told me as you were dying.

Your name, old friend, is Domovoi.

IT'S TRUE. IT'S ALL TRUE. I REMEMBER EVERYTHING.

E LOWER ELEMENTS.

KOBOI'S SHUTTLE—
NCEPT MODEL THAT
R WENT INTO MASS
PUCTION. ITS OUTER
IS STEALTH ORE AND
FOIL.

PST—
SOLUTELY
ORBITANT.

SECURE THE PRISONERS IN THE PASSENGER BAY AND GET ME A FACE LINK TO GIOVANNI ZITO IN SICILY.

AT ONCE, MISTRESS.

CHAPTER 7: THE TEMPLE OF ARTEMIS

Belinda, my ear daughter. Is that you? When are you oming home?

YES, PAPA. IT'S ME. HOW IS EVERYTHING THERE?

Molto bene. Wonderful. The mountains are beautiful. The skiing is...

IDIOTA...

HOW IS EVERYTHING WITH THE PROBE? ARE WE ON SCHEDULE?

Yes, my dear. Everything is on schedule. The explosive ods are being buried today. The probe's systems check was a resounding success. We are on course.

EXCELLENT, PAPA. YOU ARE SO GOOD TO YOUR LITTLE BELINDA. I WILL BE WITH YOU SOON.

Hurry home, my dear.

HOW LONG TO THE THEME PARK?

WE'VE ENTERED THE MAIN CHUTE NETWORK. FIVE HOURS. MAYBE LESS.

TO GIVE HOLLY AND ARTEMIS WHAT THEY DESERVE, I THINK I CAN SPARE *FIVE* HOURS.

THE ELEVEN WONDERS THEME PARK IN HAVEN'S OLD TOWN DISTRICT.

BRAINCHILD OF A BILLIONAIRE PIXIE WHO WANTED TO CASH IN ON THE PEOPLE'S FASCINATION WITH MUD MEN.

THE PARK WAS BUILT ON CHEAP REAL ESTATE. THE TUNNELS HERE WERE DECLARED UNSAFE LONG AGO.

TEN THOUSAND YEARS OF CIVILIZATION AND YOU ONLY MANAGE TO PRODUCE ELEVEN SO-CALLED WONDERS.

YOU KNOW OF COURSE THAT THERE ARE ONLY SEVEN WONDERS ON THE OFFICIAL LIST.

YOU HUMANS ARE SO NARROW-MINDED.

I'M SURPRISED YOU'D WANT TO BE ONE, THEN.

WELL, THE FAIRY PEOPLE ARE ABOUT TO BE WIPED OUT, SO MY OPTIONS ARE SOMEWHAT LIMITED.

LET ME SHOW YOU WHERE YOU'RE GOING TO BE TORN APART.

NOW.

The creatures are frantic now as they hurl rock after rock into the shallow water.

We huddle together on our small island of rotting carcasses, waiting for the end.

"Okay, I have a plan. I stay here and fight them. You go back in the river."

"I appreciate
suicidal gestu
Holly, but the
must be anoth
way. Okay, if t
were a war ga
I'd look for
the other side
weaknesses
What are they

WATER IS ONE. AND LIGHT... TROLLS HATE LIGHT. THEY LIKE IT HERE, BECAUSE GLO-STRIPS ARE ON EMERGENCY POWER AND THE FAKE SUN IS ON MINIMUM.

IF WE COULD CLIMB UP AND GET TO THE SUN, COULD YOU USE THE POWER CELLS FROM OUR HANDCUFFS TO LIGHT IT UP AGAIN?

"Yes, I suppose so. But how do we get past the trolls?"

"That's the really smart bit. We distract them with a little television."

We turn up the brightness control on Opal's little television until it glares white light.

IF WE DON'T MAKE IT, I'M SORRY YOU DON'T REMEMBER ME. IT'S GOOD TO BE WITH A FRIEND AT A TIME LIKE THIS.

IF WE MAKE IT THROUGH THIS, WE WILL BE FRIENDS. BONDED BY TRAUMA. READY?

We reach the roof and scamper on all fours to the highest point.

Behind us, I hear angry trolls clambering up the scaffolding after us.

The plaster is white and unmarked. It looks like a field of...

Snow.

I'm having a memory.

I THINK I REMEMBER BEING IN THE ARCTIC.

WE WERE. BUT PERHAPS WE CAN TALK ABOUT IT WHEN THERE ARE NO TROLLS TRYING TO EAT US. HELP ME. I CAN'T FIND THE POWER PORT.

I'VE GOT SOMETHING. THE POWER CELLS FIT IN HERE.

HERE COME THE TROLLS, ARTEMIS. EITHER THIS WORKS, OR THIS IS GOODBYE.

Holly waits until the trolls are close and then...

The globe blasts out a blinding wall of light.

For just a moment, everything is brilliant white.

The trolls collapse, fall or run.

I HAD HOPED THE CELLS WOULD POWER THE SUN FOR LONGER. THAT SEEMS LIKE A LOT OF EFFORT FOR SUCH A BRIEF REPRIEVE.

I SUPPOSE IT TAKES A LOT OF JUICE. STILL, IT HAS BOUGHT US *SOME* TIME. YOU'RE VERY CALM ALL OF A SUDDEN.

I HAVE NO CHOICE. I HAVE ANALYZED THE SITUATION AND CONCLUDED THAT THERE IS NO WAY FOR US TO ESCAPE.

HOWEVER, I HAVE NO INTENTION OF SPENDING MY FINAL MINUTES IN HYSTERICS FOR OPAL KOBOI'S AMUSEMENT. SHE IS DOUBTLESS WATCHING, EVEN NOW.

I find myself more frustrated than scared. Julius's final order was to save Artemis and I haven't even managed to accomplish that.

I'M SORRY YOU DON'T REMEMBER JULIUS. YOU TWO ARGUED A LOT, BUT BEHIND IT ALL HE ADMIRED YOU.

BUTLER AS WELL. THOSE TWO WERE REALLY ON T SAME WAVELENGTH LIKE TWO OLD SOLDIERS.

CHAPTER 8:

SOME INTELLIGENT CONVERSATION

I find a computer in the rear of the shuttle.

I don't know if this is all real. But if there's a danger of a war between fairies and humans I have to find out.

That's what Father would do.

I take a breath and then push in the disk

Within seconds, I'm looking at myself on screen.

"How nice for you to see me. Doubtless this will be the first intelligent conversation you have had for some time."

It's a message I recorded to myself before I apparently went to Chicago to deal with a Jon Spiro.

Images flash from the screen, filling in empty spaces in my head.

I had the mirrored contact lenses made myself to avoid being mesmerized.

I put the wrong date on the search warrants for Mulch.

It's all true.

And suddenly...

I remember everything.

ot all the memories
e things I'm proud of:

I kidnapped Holly
and imprisoned her.

How could I have done that?

I know it all now.

Commander
Root is gone.
She took him
from his People.

I beat Koboi before and I will beat her again.

ere is one thought in my head,
ore persistent than all the rest.

Friends.

ARTEMIS,
ARE YOU...

I'M BACK. I REMEMBER
EVERYTHING.

I have friends.

IS COMPUTER DISK
GAVE TO MULCH TO
EEP SAFE DID THE
TRICK.

BUT THE
ONLY THING YOU
GAVE TO MULCH
WAS THE GOLD
MEDALLION.

EXACTLY.
I AM A GENIUS,
AFTER ALL.

HOLLY, I'M SO SORRY
ABOUT JULIUS. I KNOW OUR
RELATIONSHIP WAS ROCKY,
BUT I HAD NOTHING BUT
RESPECT FOR HIM.

There are tears
in Holly's eyes
and she nods.

NOW WE'RE ALL REACQUAINTED, WE NEED TO LOCATE OPAL KOBOI. SHE COULD BE ANYWHERE.

NO NEED. I KNOW EXACTLY WHERE OUR WOULD-BE WAR STARTER IS. LIKE ALL MEGALOMANIACS, SHE HAS A TENDENCY TO SHOW OFF.

OPAL REVEALED MORE OF HER PLANS THAN SHE KNEW WHEN SHE SAID HER HUMAN NAME WAS BELINDA ZITO.

IF YOU WISHED TO SOMEHOW LEAD THE HUMANS TO THE FAIRY PEOPLE, WHO BETTER TO ADOPT YOU THAN BILLIONAIRE ENVIRONMENTALIST GIOVANNI ZITO?

THERE'S BEEN A MUD MAN NAMED ZITO ALL OVER THE HUMAN NEWS CHANNELS TODAY. DO YOU THINK IT'S THE SAME ONE?

I REALLY HOPE NOT, BUT I'D BET MY LIFE IT IS.

Of course, it is.

We have sent craft into space, and yet we have no idea what is at the centre of our own planet. Today we will make history and find out.

Today, for the first time ever, we will send a probe all the way down into the outer core.

"Imagine if the currents of liquid metal in the outer core could be harnessed. There's enough free energy in that molten metal to power the world."

SO TODAY WE ARE SENDING AN UNMANNED PROBE, BRISTLING WITH SENSORS. WHATEVER IS DOWN THERE, WE WILL FIND IT.

SEVERAL LARGE CHARGES WILL BE DETONATED UNDERGROUND. THEY WILL CREATE A MILLION TONS OF MOLTEN IRON TO ALLOW THE PROBE TO DESCEND.

AND WHEN IS THIS HAPPENING, MR. ZITO?

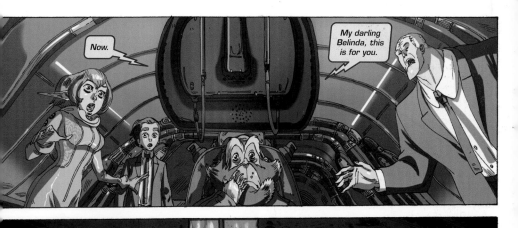

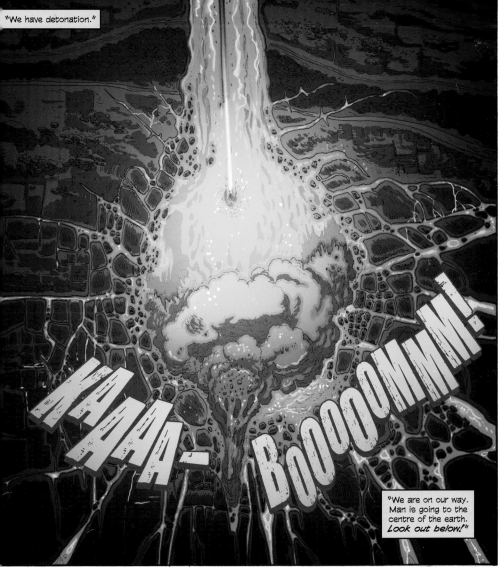

The moods in our shuttle range from glum to desolate. Our communications are down and we have no way to warn Foaly.

I HAVE NO DOUBT HE ALREADY KNOWS, HOLLY. THAT CENTAUR MONITORS ALL THE HUMAN NEWS.

I'M SURE HE DOES. BUT HE'S PLANNING FOR A CRACKPOT HUMAN SCHEME. NOT ONE BACKED UP BY OPAL'S ADVANCED FAIRY KNOWLEDGE.

I HAVE TO TURN MYSELF IN, EVEN IF I AM A MURDER SUSPECT.

YOU DO THAT AND THEY'LL LOCK YOU UP AND WE'LL NEVER STOP THAT PROBE.

ARTEMIS IS RIGHT, HOLLY.

ASK YOURSELF: WHAT WOULD COMMANDER ROOT DO?

JULIUS WOULD TAKE CARE OF OPAL KOBOI HIMSELF. YOU KNOW HE WOULD.

AND THAT'S EXACTLY WHAT WE'RE GOING TO DO.

EXCELLENT.

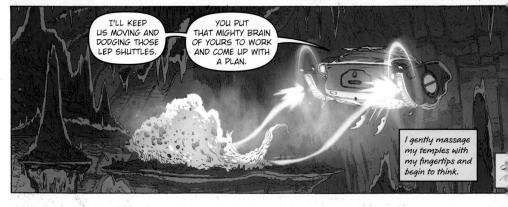

I'LL KEEP US MOVING AND DODGING THOSE LEP SHUTTLES.

YOU PUT THAT MIGHTY BRAIN OF YOURS TO WORK AND COME UP WITH A PLAN.

I gently massage my temples with my fingertips and begin to think.

ZITO EARTH FARM, CILY, ITALY.

X WEEKS AGO.

HAPTER 9:
DADDY'S GIRL

I THINK THE SPEECH WENT WELL, BUT WITH POLITICIANS WHO CAN TELL? WE'LL SEE WHAT THE NEWSPAPERS SAY TOMORROW. CIAO, PAOLA.

TSIK

WHO ARE YOU? WHAT ARE YOU DOING IN MY HOUSE?

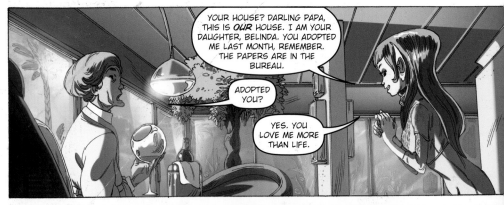

ALL OPAL WOULD HAVE TO DO TO BRING DISASTER TO HAVEN CITY IS BLOW A CRACK BETWEEN THE ORE'S PATH AND CHUTE E7. THEN THE ORE WOULD FOLLOW THE PATH OF LEAST RESISTANCE AND FLOW INTO THE CHUTE...

...AND DOWN STRAIGHT TO HAVEN CITY.

EXACTLY. MY BEST GUESS IS THAT, EVEN WITH THE BLAST WALLS, HALF THE CITY WOULD BE DESTROYED.

AND THE OTHER HALF WOULD BE LEFT BROADCASTING SIGNALS FOR THE HUMAN WORLD TO HEAR.

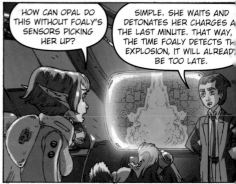

HOW CAN OPAL DO THIS WITHOUT FOALY'S SENSORS PICKING HER UP?

SIMPLE. SHE WAITS AND DETONATES HER CHARGES A THE LAST MINUTE. THAT WAY, THE TIME FOALY DETECTS TH EXPLOSION, IT WILL ALREAD BE TOO LATE.

OKAY, SO ALL WE NEED TO DO IS FIND OPAL'S CHARGES AND REMOVE THEM?

IF ONLY IT WERE THAT SIMPLE. OPAL WILL NOT TAKE ANY CHANCES WITH THINGS GOING WRONG. SHE'LL WAIT UNTIL THE LAST MINUTE TO PLANT HER CHARGES.

SO WE GET INTO THE CHUTE AND WAIT UNTIL SHE PLANTS THE CHARGES?

TOO RISKY. IF FOALY PICKS US UP ON HIS SENSORS, THEY SEND LEP SHIPS. WE'LL BE PURSUED AND ARRESTED, THANKS TO YOU MURDERING COMMANDER ROOT, REMEMBER?

BUT, ARTEMIS, SURELY EVERYONE MUST KNOW THAT OPAL HAS ESCAPED BY NOW.

THERE'S THE RUB. THAT SINGLE POINT IS THE KEY TO EVERYTHING. PEOPLE OBVIOUSLY *DON'T* KNOW OPAL HAS ESCAPED.

MY BEST GUESS WOULD BE THAT THE OPAL IN CUSTODY IS SOME KIND OF CLONE CRAFTED BY FAIRY TECHNOLOGY. ALIVE, BUT ESSENTIALLY BRAIN-DEAD.

GIOVANNI ZITO AND THE CORE PROBE

CRUST
MOHO
UPPER MANTLE
LOWER MANTLE
OUTER CORE
LIQUID-SOLID BOUNDARY
INNER CORE

NAME: Giovanni Zito

BACKGROUND: Zito is one of the most famous Italians in the world. This billionaire environmentalist first came to international fame when he jumped on the back of a humpback whale to save it from whalers' harpoons. The image became the bestselling *TIME* magazine cover of that decade.

ACHIEVEMENTS: Zito has a doctorate in alternative energy. He has spent his life and fortune developing eco-friendly solutions to modern problems, calling his approach "clean sky thinking".

PET PROJECTS IN DEVELOPMENT INCLUDE: The Core Probe Project, a way of exploring Earth's inner space, first proposed by planetary scientist professor David Stevenson.

NORMA
di VINCENZO BELLINI
Teatro Massimo Bellini
via Perrotta,12 - 95131
CATANIA (CT) ITALIA

NOR
di VINCENZO
Teatro Massimo
via Perrotta,12 -
CATANIA (CT) IT

FOALY, ARE YOU ALL RIGHT? I MEAN AFTER THE THING WITH HOLLY SHORT AND COMMANDER ROOT? I KNOW YOU WERE CLOSE TO THEM.

OF COURSE I'M ALL RIGHT. WHY WOULDN'T I BE ALL RIGHT? JUST BECAUSE TWO OF MY BEST FRIENDS ARE DEAD AND ONE IS ACCUSED OF MURDERING THE OTHER? I'M OBVIOUSLY FINE.

CHAPTER 10: HORSE SENSE

LET'S JUST CONCENTRATE ON THE PROBE, SHALL WE, ROOB?

SORRY, SIR. THE PROBE IS NOW DOWN TO SIXTY-TWO MILES. I CAN'T BELIEVE THE HUMANS HAVE GOT THIS FAR.

I CAN'T BELIEVE IT EITHER, BUT THEY HAVE.

KEEP A CLOSE EYE ON IT. ESPECIALLY WHEN IT RUNS PARALLEL TO CHUTE E7. I DON'T EXPECT TROUBLE, BUT JUST IN CASE.

YES SIR. OH, AND WE HAVE CAPTAIN VERBIL ON LINE TWO, FROM THE SURFACE.

CHIX, STOP HOVERING AND COME DOWN WHERE I CAN SEE YOU.

Sorry. I'm still a bit emotional from Commander Kelp's grilling. Listen, I have a message for you from Mulch Diggums.

GO ON, THEN. TELL ME WHAT OUR FOULMOUTHED FRIEND THINKS OF ME.

This is just between us, right? I don't want this getting around.

YES, CHIX. IT'S JUST BETWEEN US.

Is this a high-security line?

YES, JUST TELL ME WHAT HE SAID!

Opal Koboi is back.

That's what he sai

HA—OPAL ISN'T BACK. DON'T MAKE ME LAUGH. I'M LOOKING AT HER LIVE FEED RIGHT NOW.

SHE'S IN THE ARGON CLINIC, SUSPENDED IN HER COMA HARNESS, AND SHE HAD A DNA SWAB TEST A FEW MINUTES AGO.

I DON'T BLAME YOU FOR BEING TAKEN IN, CHIX. MULCH HAS FOOLED SMARTER SPRITES THAN YOU.

Hey, there's no need for that. I have feelings too, you know.

Anyway, it could be true. You could be wrong. It is possible, you know. Maybe Opal Koboi conned you.

Mulch seemed so sincere. I actually thought Holly was in danger.

WHAT? MULCH SAID HOLLY WAS IN DANGER? BUT HOLLY IS GONE. SHE DIED.

I guess Mulch was shovelling more horse dung.

HOLD THE FOR ROOB. I'M GOIN TO VISIT AN OL FRIEND.

UNCHARTED CHUTE, THREE MILES BELOW SOUTHERN ITALY.

We make good time to the surface. Now for Opal.

TELL ME AGAIN, ARTEMIS. IF WE WANT TO FIND OPAL'S STEALTH SHUTTLE, WHY ARE WE LOOKING FOR EMPTY SPACES?

OUR SENSORS ARE NOWHERE NEAR SOPHISTICATED ENOUGH TO SPOT OPAL'S STEALTH SHUTTLE. BUT I THINK THERE IS A WAY...

OUR AIR IS MADE UP OF VARIOUS GASES, OF COURSE. GASES LIKE OXYGEN, HYDROGEN AND SO ON. BUT—AND HERE'S MY POINT—THE STEALTH SHUTTLE'S HULL WILL PREVENT ANY OF THESE FROM BEING DETECTED.

SO IF WE FIND A SMALL PATCH OF SPACE WITHOUT THE USUAL AMBIENT GASES, THEN...

...THEN THAT HOLE IN THE AIR IS THE STEALTH SHUTTLE.

EXACTLY.

IF WE ASSUME THAT THE STEALTH SHUTTLE IS GOING TO BE VERY CLOSE TO CHUTE E7, THAT'S STILL A LOT OF GROUND TO SCAN, BUT LET'S TRY.

Three gas anomalies located.

THAT'S PROBABLY AN AIRPORT. LOTS OF EXHAUST FUMES.

THAT VACUUM IS PROBABLY A COMPUTER PLANT ON THE SURFACE.

AH, THERE...

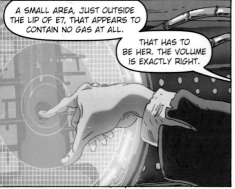

A SMALL AREA, JUST OUTSIDE THE LIP OF E7, THAT APPEARS TO CONTAIN NO GAS AT ALL.

THAT HAS TO BE HER. THE VOLUME IS EXACTLY RIGHT.

YOU REALIZE THAT AS SOON AS WE MOVE INTO THE MAIN CHUTE FOALY WILL SPOT US AND WE'LL BE OUTLAWS?

LET'S HOPE WE CAN SAVE HAVEN CITY SO WE CAN KEEP BEING OUTLAWS. AT LEAST FOR NOW.

THE ARGON CLINIC, HAVEN CITY.

THIS IS OUTRAGEOUS. WHO KNOWS WHAT EFFECT YOUR DEVICES MIGHT HAVE ON HER RECOVERING PSYCHE? I UTTERLY FORBID IT.

I DO HOPE YOU'RE NOT THINKING OF OPAL AS YOUR PERSONAL POSSESSION, DR. ARGON. SHE IS A STATE PRISONER, AND I CAN HAVE HER MOVED OUT OF HERE ANY TIME I LIKE.

MAYBE FIVE MINUTE WOULDN'T HURT.

WHAT HAVE YOU GOT THERE, ANYWAY?

DON'T WORRY. IT'S JUST A RETIMAGER.

EVERY IMAGE IS RECORDED ON THE RETINAS. THIS LEAVES A TRAIL OF MICROSCOP SCRATCHES THAT CAN BE ENHANCED AN READ. MY OWN INVENTION.

SO YOU CAN TELL US THE LAST THING THAT OPAL SAW. WHAT GOOD WILL THAT DO?

WE SHALL SEE.

OOH LOOK, SOME DARK SMUDGES.

SHALL I CALL THE NETWORKS? OR SHALL I JUST FAINT?

COMPUTER, LIGHTEN IMAGE AND ENHANCE AND WE SHOULD SEE...

SHE SAW HERSELF FROM THE SIDE. THAT MEANS THERE WERE TWO OPAL KOBOIS. TWO. THE REAL ONE THAT YOU LET ESCAPE AND THIS SHELL HERE.

"OH DEAR" HARDLY COVERS IT.

OH DEAR.

MAYBE NOW WOULD BE A GOOD TIM TO CALL THE NETWORKS, OR FAINT IN AWE.

CRRRUNCH

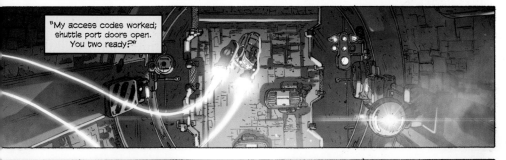

"My access codes worked; shuttle port doors open. You two ready?"

WE'RE READY, HOLLY. FLY IN A GRID SEARCH PATTERN AS THOUGH WE'RE NOT CERTAIN WHERE THE STEALTH SHUTTLE IS.

NOW, OLD FRIEND, CAN YOU MAKE CERTAIN THAT OPAL IS LOOKING THIS WAY?

BOOOOMMMMM!!

"I bet that got her attention."

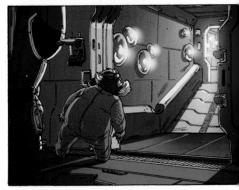

Mulch is waiting at the rendezvous site and Butler hauls him in.

I GOT WHAT YOU WANTED, MUD BOY. AND BEFORE YOU ASK, YES, I LEFT THE RADIO.

EXCELLENT. THEN WE NEED TO GET MOVING; OPAL WILL BE AFTER US ANY SECOND.

Everything depends on the next few minutes.

IF THIS IS GOING TO WORK, WE NEED TO KEEP OPAL DISTRACTED SO SHE DOESN'T DISCOVER THE TRUTH. THAT'S UP TO YOU, HOLLY.

DON'T WORRY, ARTEMIS; IT'S NOT OFTE I GET TO DO SOME FANC FLYING. OPAL WILL BE SO BUSY TRYING TO CAT US SHE WON'T HAVE TIME FOR ANYTHING ELSE.

HEAD DOWN THE CHUTE. WE MUST GET NEAR ENOUGH TO DETONATE THE CHARGES THEY'VE STOLEN. EVEN IF WE MISS THE PROBE WINDOW, AT LEAST WE CAN DESTROY ANY WITNESSES AGAINST ME.

COMPUTER SAYS THREE MINUTES UNTIL WE'RE IN DETONATION RANGE, MISTRESS.

IF WE CAN BLOW THEM UP IN THE RIGHT SECTION OF TUNNEL, MY PLAN TO DESTROY HAVEN CITY STILL MIGHT WORK.

AS SOON AS WE HIT ONE HUNDRED AND FIVE MILES UNDERGROUND, SEND THE DETONATE SIGNAL. WE MIGHT GET LUCKY.

insides feel like they're trying
orce their way out through my
oat. I'm not the only one.

IS ALL THIS JIGGLING ABOUT REALLY NECESSARY? I'VE HAD A LOT TO EAT RECENTLY, EVEN FOR A DWARF.

WE'RE AT A DEPTH OF ONE ZERO FIVE NOW. OPAL WILL BE TRYING TO DETONATE. SHE'S CLOSING FAST.

WE'RE NEARLY THERE, MULCH. TELL BUTLER TO OPEN THE BAG.

AY...ARE YOU RE OPAL WILL WHAT SHE'S SUPPOSED TO?

OF COURSE I AM. IT'S HUMAN NATURE AND OPAL IS A HUMAN NOW, REMEMBER? OKAY, HOLLY. PULL OVER.

OU'RE NOT GOING BELIEVE THIS, OP— MISS KOBOI.

DON'T TELL ME THEY'VE STOPPED?

YES, THEY ARE HOVERING AT A HUNDRED AND TWENTY-FOUR MILES. WHY WOULD THEY DO THAT?

JUST KEEP SENDING THE DETONATION SIGNAL SO WE CAN...

AH, HERE WE GO. THEY'RE GETTING IN TOUCH.

Opal, I am giving you one chance to surrender. We have disarmed your charges and the LEP are on their way. Turn yourself over to Captain Short.

But if it doesn't...

NO. NO. NO. NO.

...Opal seals her own fate.

I'VE BEEN TRICKED! HOW COULD THIS HAPPEN? EJECTOR SEATS. WE HAVE TEN SECONDS.

WHAT?

The charges detonate uselessly at seventy-four and a half miles.

That's well above the parallel stretch.

Haven City is safe.

olly pulls our shuttle close
the chute wall to avoid the
iling debris, but it's not over.

THOSE TWO DOTS
ARE ESCAPE PODS,
BUT...OH NO.

THE OTHER TWO AREN'T.
OPAL HAS LAUNCHED TWO
HEAT-SEEKING MISSILES AND
THEY'RE HEADING STRAIGHT
FOR US.

should have expected this.
stare at the screen and
wish I could destroy the
missiles by concentration.

While I think, Holly acts.
She turns off the engines.

We fall like a stone.

The rushing air cools
the engines and our
heat signature drops.

Butler uses foam from
the fire extinguishers
to help cool the engines.

Two seconds
to impact...

And I see the missiles
veer away from us.

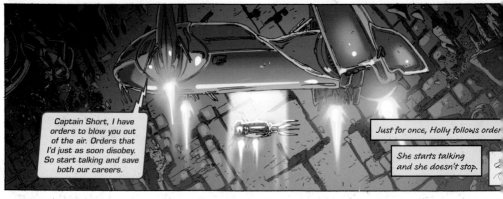

CHAPTER 11: **THE LAST GOODBYE**

"We think we know what happened...

"Opal's escape capsule limped to the surface, leaking plasma as it went.

"She made it almost ten miles across country before she ditched in a vineyard."

THESE VINES ARE ALL I HAVE.

I'M ALONE. WHO ARE YOU TO CRASH YOUR LITTLE AEROPLANE AND DESTROY THEM?

YOU HAVE ME NOW. I AM YOUR DAUGHTER, BELINDA.

I HAVE A DAUGHTER? WELL, THEN GET A SHOVEL AND CLEAN UP THIS MESS OR YOU'LL GO TO BED HUNGRY.

"Judging from the satellite images, we think that was the moment her fairy magic ran out."

I DON'T DO PHYSICAL WORK. YOU WILL SERVE ME.

THAT IS NOW YOUR PURPOSE IN LIFE.

DON'T SPEAK SUCH POISON. NOW PICK UP YOUR SHOVEL AND WORK. *WORK!*

"By the time the LEP retrieval team get there, I bet she'll be almost happy to see them."

COMMANDER ROOT'S RECYCLING CEREMONY.

Of all the things Sool has done to me, this is the worst.

Everyone knows I'm innocent, but, until the Tribunal actually votes, I'm officially a murder suspect.

So I'm all the way up here. Under armed guard.

While down there, they say goodbye to Julius Root.

LATER.

YOU'RE CLEAR. THE TRIBUNAL VOTED SEVEN TO ONE IN YOUR FAVOUR.

LET ME GUESS WHO VOTED AGAINST.

YOU MAY HAVE ESCAPED THIS CHARGE, BUT I'LL BE WATCHING YOU LIKE A HAWK FROM NOW ON, SHORT.

HEY, WHAT ABOUT ME, PONY BOY?

THERE'S NO MEDAL, BUT, AS YOU HELPED SAVE THE CITY, THE TRIBUNAL DECIDED YOU'RE A FREE DWARF.

YES!

THE LAST THING JULIUS EVER TOLD ME WAS THAT MY JOB WAS TO SERVE THE PEOPLE AND THAT I SHOULD DO THAT ANY WAY I COULD.

SMART FAIRY. I DO HOPE YOU INTEND HONOURING THOSE WORDS.

I DO. BUT WITH YOU LOOKING OVER MY SHOULDER WAITING FOR A MISTAKE I WON'T BE ABLE TO HELP ANYONE. SO I'M GOING IT ALONE.

I QUIT.

NO, HOLLY! THE FORCE NEEDS YOU. I NEED YOU.

DON'T WORRY, OLD FRIEND. I WON'T BE FAR AWAY.

HEY, MULCH. ONCE WE GET AN OFFICE TO RENT, WE'LL BE THE BEST PRIVATE DETECTIVES UNDER THE WORLD.

PRIVATE DETECTIVES. I LIKE IT. HEY, I'M NOT A SIDEKICK, AM I? BECAUSE THE SIDEKICK ALWAYS GETS IT.

CONGRATULATIONS, COMMANDER SOOL. YOU'VE JUST MANAGED TO ALIENATE THE LEP'S FINEST OFFICER.

SEND THEM HOME. NOW.

OWL MANOR.

I come to gradually in my room.

And remember a tranquilizer dart hitting my neck.

I feel well and rested, and with all my memories in place. Then again, if they weren't— how would I know?

...r a few minutes I have ...e luxury of just thinking.

My favourite occupation.

Which way will my life go from here? It's up to me. What should I do with the stolen "Fairy Thief" painting?

...mething ...rates in my ...ket pocket. ...s a fairy ...mmunicator.

HELLO, HOLLY. I'M GUESSING YOU SLIPPED ME THIS LITTLE DEVICE?

You got home safely? Sorry about the sedatives. Sool is a pig.

Mulch and I have got our first client. He's an art dealer who's had a picture stolen. You interested in a little consultancy work?

AS LONG AS YOU TELL ME WHERE TO SEND THE BILL.

Some things never change.

...tler bursts through ...e door, gun in hand.

ARTEMIS, ARE YOU...

I'M FINE, OLD FRIEND. I'M TALKING TO HOLLY.

I hear car tyres crunch on the drive.